STEP INTO 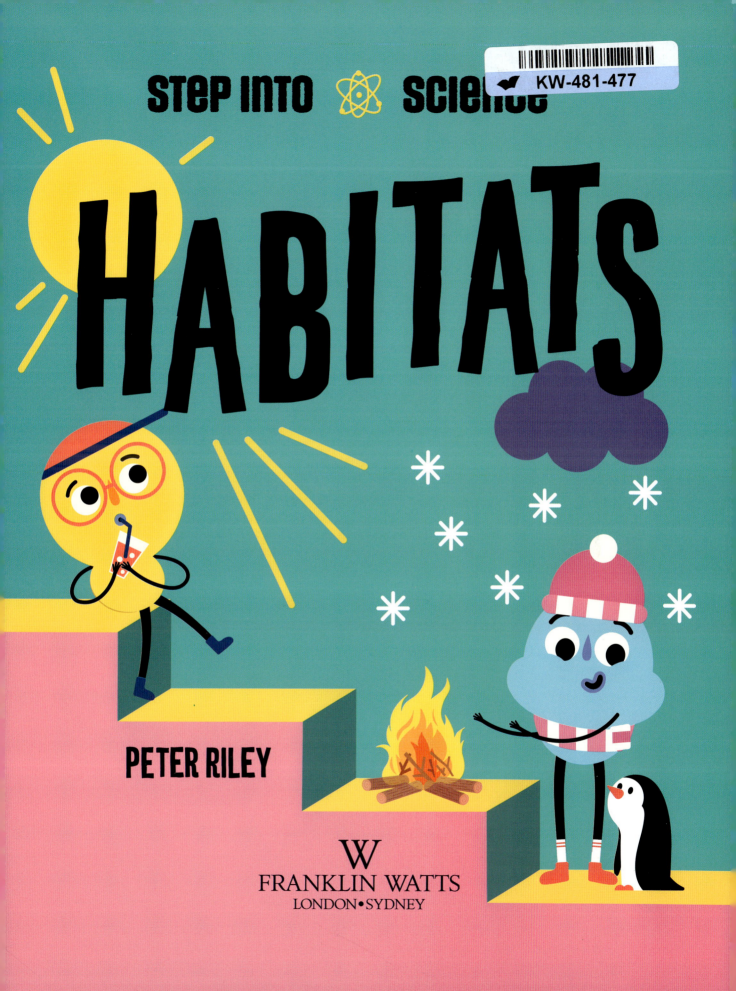 SCIENCE

HABITATS

PETER RILEY

W
FRANKLIN WATTS
LONDON•SYDNEY

To my granddaughter, Holly Jane.

First published in Great Britain in 2022 by Hodder & Stoughton

Text copyright © Peter Riley 2015

Design and illustration copyright © Hodder & Stoughton Ltd 2022

The text in this book was previously published in the series *Moving Up with Science*.

HB ISBN: 978 1 4451 8320 6

PB ISBN: 978 1 4451 8319 0

Editor: Elise Short
Design and Illustration: Collaborate Ltd

Every attempt has been made to clear copyright. Should there be any inadvertent omission, please apply to the Publishers for rectification.

Printed in China

Franklin Watts
An imprint of
Hachette Children's Group
Part of Hodder & Stoughton
Carmelite House
50 Victoria Embankment
London EC4Y 0DZ

An Hachette UK Company
www.hachettechildrens.co.uk

CONTENTS

What is a habitat? 4

Plant groups 6

Identifying living things 8

Animal groups 10

Habitats in spring 12

Habitats in summer 14

Habitats in autumn 16

Habitats in winter 18

Water habitats 20

Habitats across the world 22

Humans and habitats 24

Saving habitats 26

Glossary 28

Answers to the activities and questions 30

Further information 31

Index 32

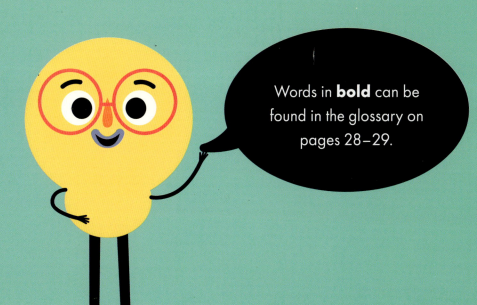

Words in **bold** can be found in the glossary on pages 28–29.

WHAT IS A HABITAT?

A habitat is the home of a living thing. It is the place where a plant or an animal gets everything it needs to survive and **breed**. There are many different kinds of habitat. They can be as small as the space under a stone or as large as a forest.

PLANT HABITATS

Plants need water, soil, light and warmth to make food and grow so they can breed and produce a plant **population** in the habitat.

Rocks beside a woodland stream provide mosses with a shady and damp habitat in which to grow.

FOOD CHAINS

Scientists link plants and animals together into **food chains**. A food chain shows how food energy passes from one living thing to another in a habitat.

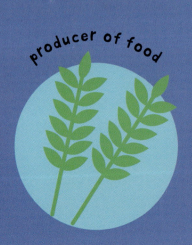
producer of food

ANIMAL HABITATS

Animals need places to shelter from bad weather and to hide away from **predators**. They also need plenty of food in their habitat. **Herbivores** feed on plants, so they live in a habitat where plenty of plants grow. **Carnivores** feed on other animals so they need a habitat with plenty of animals. **Omnivores** need a habitat with plenty of plants and animals because they feed on both.

Many fish live around a **coral reef** habitat because it is a good place to hide from predators and food can be found easily there.

herbivore

carnivore

In this food chain a plant is eaten by a mouse. The mouse is then eaten by an owl.

PLANT GROUPS

To make plants easier to **identify** in their habitat they are divided into four groups: mosses, ferns, conifers and flowering plants.

MOSSES

Mosses are small green plants. They grow **stalks** with swollen tips, which let out **spores** into the air. When the spores settle on the ground they grow into new moss plants.

FERNS

Ferns have huge feathery leaves called **fronds**. On the underside of the leaves are rows of green or brown swellings that make spores. The spores escape into the air, settle on the soil and grow into new plants.

These mosses and ferns can be found growing in a shady, damp rocky habitat.

CONIFERS

Conifers are trees with long, needle-shaped leaves which most of them keep all year round. They grow woody **cones** which produce **seeds** that are blown away on the wind. Conifers are able to live in dry cold habitats.

Conifers are often found growing in mountainous habitats.

FLOWERING PLANTS

There are two kinds of flowering plant: non-woody and woody. Non-woody or **herbaceous** plants cannot grow in cold weather and die back into the soil in winter. Woody plants include trees and bushes. Most woody plants are **deciduous**. This means that they lose their leaves in the autumn and grow new ones in the spring.

A bright, warm day helps trees and bluebells grow in this woodland habitat.

IDENTIFYING LIVING THINGS

When scientists study living things in a habitat, they first need to identify them. One way is to use a **key**. It contains the different **features** of a group of living things. These are set out as a series of questions so that you can use the key to identify exactly which plant or animal you are looking at.

IDENTIFY PLANTS IN A HABITAT

You can make a key to identify plants by looking at and comparing their leaves. Look for plants on a patch of grass.

1.

Look for daisies, buttercups, clover and dandelions.

2.

Study each flower in turn and follow the stalk back to find a leaf attached to it.

CHECK THE LEAF SHAPE

Look at the shape of the plant's leaf. You may find that some leaves are divided into three or more leafy parts. These parts are called **leaflets**. Now look at the leaf's edges. You may find that the edges are smooth or have little points.

DIVIDE INTO GROUPS

Divide the plants into those with leaflets and those without leaflets. Divide each of these groups into those with smooth edges and those with pointy edges. Arrange all this information as questions and connect them by lines to make a key.

USING THE KEY

The key is read by starting at the top, reading a question, comparing it with the leaf and moving along the lines until the leaf matches the one described in the key. When they match, you can identify the plant.

KEY FOR LAWN PLANTS

Is the leaf divided into leaflets?

leaf divided into leaflets

leaf not divided into leaflets

leaflets with smooth edges
CLOVER

leaflets with pointy edges
BUTTERCUP

leaf with smooth edges
DAISY

leaf with pointy edges
DANDELION

ANIMAL GROUPS

To make animals easier to identify in their habitat, they are divided into two big groups: invertebrates and vertebrates. Vertebrates are animals that have a skeleton of bone or **cartilage**; invertebrates are animals that do not.

INVERTEBRATES

EARTHWORMS

are animals with long, thin bodies divided into **segments**. Habitat: soil.

MOLLUSCS

such as slugs and snails, have soft bodies without segments. Habitats: low woodland plants and spaces under stones.

SPIDERS

have eight legs. Habitats: the ground, tall flowering plants, bushes and trees.

INSECTS

have hard outer bodies and six legs. Habitats: the ground, woodland plants, bushes and trees.

SUB-GROUPS

Each of these big groups is divided into smaller sub-groups according to the animals' other **characteristics**. Each animal characteristic helps it to live and grow in a particular type of habitat.

AMPHIBIANS

such as newts and frogs, have a tadpole stage that lives in water and an adult stage that lives on land. They have smooth skin.
Habitats: ponds, plants near water, under stones.

VERTEBRATES

FISH

live in water. They have **scales** and fins.
Habitats: seas, rivers, lakes and ponds.

REPTILES

have scales and lay soft-shelled eggs on land.
Habitats: fields, woodlands, deserts, rivers and seas.

MAMMALS

have fur. They make milk to feed their young.
Habitats: woodlands, fields, deserts, riverbanks and seas.

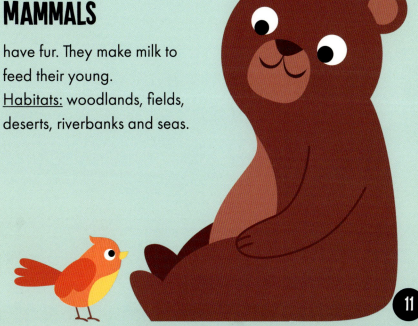

BIRDS

have feathers and wings. They lay hard-shelled eggs in nests.
Habitats: woodlands, trees and fields; beside ponds, lakes, rivers and seas.

HABITATS IN SPRING

In many habitats there are four seasons in the year. These are spring, summer, autumn and winter. In spring the weather becomes warmer after the cold winter. This change affects the plants and animals living in the habitat.

PLANTS

In early spring, some herbaceous plants, such as bluebells, start to grow new **shoots**. Their leaves spread out to catch the sunlight. The plants use the sunlight to make food to grow their flowers.

The flowers attract insects for **pollination**. The flower's pollen sticks to the insect, which moves it to another flower of the same kind so seeds and fruits can be made.

BIRDS

During the spring, male birds sing or **display** to attract female birds. When a female joins a male they form a pair. They often build their nest in trees, far away from predators. The female lays a **clutch** of eggs and the pair often takes turns at keeping them warm until they hatch.

A European robin sits on her nest to keep her eggs warm and safe. The eggs will hatch in 12 to 14 days.

MAMMALS

In winter some mammals, such as bats, hide away in a sheltered place and sleep. This is called **hibernation** and it keeps them safe from the cold winter weather. They wake up when the warm spring weather arrives and begin to feed and search for **mates**.

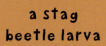

a stag beetle larva

INSECTS

An insect can spend winter as an egg, a **pupa** or a hibernating adult. In spring, the insect eggs hatch and the **larvae** begin to feed. The pupa breaks open and an adult insect climbs out while other adult insects come out of hibernation.

HABITATS IN SUMMER

During the warm summer months, habitats are full of activity. More flowers grow and animals spend time feeding and looking after their young.

PLANTS

In late spring and early summer, the **buds** on deciduous trees swell up, then burst open. The leaves of the trees make it too shady for the spring flowering plants below them, such as snowdrops, so they die back. Through the summer more herbaceous plants grow their shoots and flowers.

INSECTS

Many insects, such as flies and some butterflies, go through their whole **life cycle** from egg to larva, then pupa to adult, in the spring and summer.

pupa

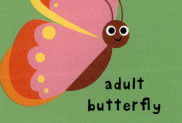

adult butterfly

BIRDS

When the weather is warm enough, a bird's eggs hatch. A bird will feed its chicks until they can feed themselves. Some birds, such as robins, go on to lay another clutch of eggs and raise more chicks before the end of the summer.

MAMMALS

During spring and summer, mammals lose their thick hair and grow a thinner coat to keep them cool in the warmer weather. The mammals that have found a mate in the spring give birth and then **rear** their young.

The female deer rears her young fawn near long grass and trees to protect it from predators.

USE THE INFORMATION ON THIS PAGE TO DRAW A PICTURE OF THE ANIMAL AND PLANT LIFE IN A LOCAL HABITAT IN SUMMER. INCLUDE LABELS.

HABITATS IN AUTUMN

In the autumn, plants and animals in a habitat get ready for cold weather. Animals store food. Herbaceous plant stems turn yellow and brown. The leaves of deciduous trees turn yellow, orange and red.

READY FOR WINTER

Mammals, such as squirrels, make stores of nuts in the autumn to use up through the winter. Male deer, called stags, grow **antlers**. They look for female hinds, so that the two can breed and have their young in the spring. Stags attract hinds by calling out to them and showing off their antlers.

Stags compete for a hind. This behaviour is called rutting.

SPREADING SPORES

Fungi grow threads in the soil to feed off dead leaves and shoots. Then they grow the stalks and caps we call toadstools and mushrooms. Fungi reproduce by releasing tiny spores into the air. The wind spreads the spores, which form new threads in the soil of the woodland floor.

Fungi caps open like umbrellas and spread their tiny spores into the air.

PLANTS

In autumn, many plants' fruits ripen. Fruits contain seeds that need to be spread so new plants can grow the following spring. Soft and watery fruits, like blackberries, are eaten by animals. Their seeds pass through the animals' bodies and come out whole in their **dung**. Some trees make nuts, which contain seeds. These are spread by birds and squirrels.

The leaves of deciduous trees change colour and fall from the trees.

DESCRIBE THE PLANTS AND ANIMALS THAT LIVE AND GROW IN YOUR AREA AND THE LOCAL HABITAT IN AUTUMN. HOW DO THEY CHANGE THROUGH THE SEASON?

HABITATS IN WINTER

During winter, many plants die back. Lots of animals grow a thick coat or they hibernate to protect themselves from the cold. Some birds **migrate** to warmer habitats.

PLANTS

Bark protects trees and shrubs from cold winter weather. Herbaceous plants survive as seeds, roots, **bulbs** or underground stems in the soil. Deciduous trees lose all of their leaves to save water and energy during the winter.

only evergreen plants, such as pines, holly and ivy, keep their leaves in winter.

INSECTS

Most adult insects die at the end of autumn but some, such as the red admiral butterfly, hide away and hibernate as adults through the winter. Some insect eggs and pupa survive the winter in the soil, or in cracks in the bark of trees.

Canada geese migrate from northern to southern America for the winter.

BIRDS

By winter young birds may live alone or gather in **flocks** with their parents and other birds. Some birds, such as warblers, fly away to warmer places to spend the winter. This seasonal movement from one place to another is called migration. Other birds, such as waxwings, migrate into the woods in winter where the trees provide protection from the cold.

MAMMALS

Many mammals eat plenty of food in autumn to help them survive the winter when food might be scarce. Bats use up this food as they hibernate. Other animals, such as squirrels, eat the nuts they stored in autumn through the winter. They forget about some stores and the seeds in the nuts grow into plants in the following spring.

Some mammals, such as foxes, do not hibernate. They grow a thicker coat of fur to keep them warm.

LIST SOME OF THE WAYS ANIMALS PREPARE TO SURVIVE THE WINTER.

WATER HABITATS

Water habitats are divided into saltwater habitats and **freshwater** habitats. Saltwater habitats include large oceans and smaller seas. Freshwater habitats include rivers, streams, lakes and ponds.

Fish, shrimps and other animals feed on **microscopic** plankton like these.

SALTWATER

The largest water habitats are the oceans. They cover nearly three-quarters of the Earth's surface. The sunlit top layer of the oceans is home to tiny plants called plant **plankton**.

On rocky shores, there are plants known as seaweed. Invertebrates, such as sea urchins, periwinkles and limpets, feed on seaweed.

RIVERS AND STREAMS

In the hills, river water moves quickly. It washes away mud and leaves the river bottom covered in pebbles. Insects such as caddisfly larvae and mayfly nymphs (young mayfly) may live under the pebbles. On flat plains near the sea, the river water flows more slowly and mud settles on the bottom. This is the habitat of worms and freshwater mussels, which burrow into the mud.

LAKES AND PONDS

In lakes and ponds the water does not move, although the wind may blow waves across the water's surface. The open water contains plankton. The edges have water plants, such as reeds, and in shallow water there may be pondweed and water lilies. Snails and leeches live on the plants, while diving beetles and fish swim around them.

Small mammals, such as voles and otters, and wading birds feed on the fish in lakes and ponds.

Mayflies lay their eggs on the surface of the water. Nymphs hatch out and swim to the safety of the rocks and pebbles on the river bed.

HABITATS ACROSS THE WORLD

The weather varies across the world and this makes different land habitats, as shown on this map. Each habitat supports different food chains.

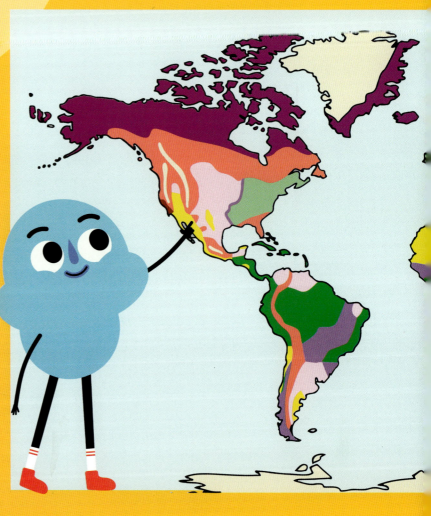

The polar regions are cold, with long, dark winters so few plants grow there.

A polar region food chain: plankton is eaten by fish, the fish are eaten by seals and the seals are eaten by polar bears.

The tundra is cool all year round but has a sunny summer, so some plants grow there.

A tundra food chain: reindeer eat the plants and wolves eat reindeer.

The coniferous forest has enough warmth and sunshine in summer for tall coniferous trees to grow.

A coniferous forest food chain: squirrels eat the seeds from the conifer's cones and great horned owls eat the squirrels.

Scrubland is largely found around the Mediterranean Sea where the summers are hot and the winters are mild.

A scrubland food chain: insects eat plants, frogs eat the insects, snakes eat the frogs.

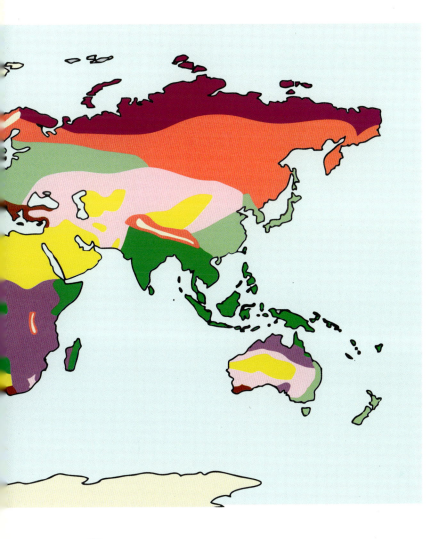

Tropical grasslands grow where there are seasons of hot; wet and hot; dry weather.

A tropical grassland food chain: zebras feed on grass and trees, hyenas eat the zebras.

Deserts have very little rainfall and only a short season when plants can grow.

A desert food chain: locusts eat the plants and the desert fox eats the locusts.

The temperate forest is made up of woodlands.

A temperate forest food chain: mice eat nuts and berries and owls eat mice.

Temperate grasslands grow where there are seasons of warm; wet and warm; dry weather.

A temperate grassland food chain: saiga antelope eat grass. The antelope are eaten by wolves.

The rainforest has hot, wet and sunny weather, which allows trees to grow to a large size.

A rainforest food chain: monkeys feed on fruits and eagles feed on the monkeys.

HUMANS AND HABITATS

About 200,000 years ago, the first people on Earth lived by hunting animals and gathering berries, nuts and roots. They moved around in their habitat so they did not take too much food from any particular place or clear areas for buildings.

FARMS AND TOWNS

About 10,000 years ago, people began clearing habitats to make farms. In time, towns were set up to **trade** crops and animals for other goods. More habitats were cleared to make room for town buildings and roads. Many plants and animals from these habitats died as they had nowhere to live, but some changed and adapted to their new habitat in the town. For example, foxes have been able to survive in towns by taking food from people's rubbish.

MINING

Habitats are often cleared for mines, where coal and metal **ores** are dug out of the ground. Coal, oil and **gas** are burnt at power stations to make electricity. Metals are used to make many things including cars, furniture and cutlery.

CLIMATE CHANGE

Every habitat has certain types of weather through the year. This yearly weather is called climate. Power stations, cars, lorries and aircraft burn **fuel**. This makes a gas called carbon dioxide. Too much carbon dioxide in the air in Earth's **atmosphere** makes the air hold onto more of the Sun's heat. The warmer air is causing **climate change** in all habitats.

Habitats are still being cleared to make room for farms, towns, cities, roads, railways and airports.

WHY DIDN'T EARLY PEOPLE CHANGE THEIR HABITAT? HOW ARE HABITATS BEING CHANGED TODAY?

SAVING HABITATS

All the plants and animals on Earth live in habitats. If these habitats are destroyed, the plants and animals in them have to learn to live in a new habitat or they will die. To keep all the different kinds of animals and plants on Earth, habitats must be protected.

USE LESS FUEL

We can all help habitats by burning less of the fuels that warm up the atmosphere. We can use less electricity by switching off lights and other electrical equipment when we are not using them. We can walk more and use cars less. Cars burn the fuels that make carbon dioxide. This warms the atmosphere and creates fumes that lead to air **pollution**.

VISIT NATURE RESERVES

In many countries people can pay to visit nature reserves where mining and chopping down trees are not allowed. Hunting animals is also banned.

The money spent by visitors helps to fund the work of nature reserves.

RECYCLE

When materials, such as the metal in drinks cans, are recycled, they are changed and used again. This reduces the amount of habitats being destroyed for metal ore mining. Recycling also means less energy is used to make new things and there is less rubbish to find space for.

clearing litter in your area is an easy way to help protect animals and plants.

CLEAR AWAY RUBBISH

Habitats are often damaged by litter. Animals can cut themselves on glass or choke on plastic. Rubbish covers plants and stops light reaching them so they eventually die. We can all help by clearing litter away from our parks and gardens, and by putting up posters to warn of the dangers of litter.

CREATE NEW HABITATS

We can help to protect habitats by creating ponds with lots of water plants to attract animals. We can plant trees, bushes and flowers in our gardens and include nest boxes to attract birds and boxes to provide a roosting place for bats.

GLOSSARY

Antler one of two horns on a deer's head.

Bark the material that covers the trunk and branches of a tree or bush.

Breed to produce young. Plants and animals do this in many different ways.

Bud a swelling on a stem in which a leaf or flower grows.

Bulb the swollen underground stem of a plant.

Carnivore an animal that only eats other animals.

Cartilage a strong tissue between bones that stops them grinding together.

Characteristic a feature of a plant or animal that helps it survive in a habitat.

Climate change the change in the weather at a place over a number of years. When a habitat's climate changes, the animals and plants there have to change and adapt to the new temperature and weather conditions or they will die.

Clutch the number of eggs laid and cared for at one time.

Cone a woody case containing seeds made by conifers.

Coral reef a huge stony structure that is made of millions of coral animals called polyps.

Deciduous a tree or bush which loses its leaves for part of the year.

Display when an animal or bird shows its feathers or performs a dance to attract a mate.

Dung animal droppings.

Evergreen a tree or bush which has leaves on its branches all through the year.

Feature the part of a plant or animal that can be used to identify it, such as the shape of the leaf or colour of its fur.

Flock a group of animals, such as sheep or any bird.

Food chain a line of living things linked together to show how food energy passes from one to the next.

Freshwater water that does not contain salt.

Frond a huge leaf that grow out of a fern from close to the ground.

Fuel a material that can provide energy, usually by burning it.

Fungus a living thing that has tiny threads that feed on dead plants and animals. It often grows stalks and caps to spread its spores.

Gas a material that has no fixed shape or volume, which flows and can be squashed.

Herbaceous a group of plants with shoots that die back after making fruits.

Herbivore an animal that only eats plants.

Hibernating when animals sleep through the winter.

Identify to find out the name of something, such as a plant or an animal.

Key in science, a set of information or series of questions that can be used to identify a plant or animal.

Larva the stage in an insect's life after the egg, such as a caterpillar or a grub, that grows and changes into a pupa.

Leaflet a small leaf which forms part of a larger leaf.

Life cycle the stages in the life of a plant or animal.

Mate the partner of animals pairing up to breed.

Microscopic an object so small it can only be seen using a scientific instrument called a microscope.

Migrate to move from one habitat to another because of a change in the seasons.

Omnivore an animal that eats both plants and animals.

Ore a rock containing metal, which is released when the rock is heated.

Plankton tiny plants and animals that live in the seas, oceans, lakes and ponds.

Pollination the movement of pollen from one flower to another flower of the same kind.

Pollution the presence of something harmful or poisonous in the air or water.

Population a group of the same kind of animal or plant.

Predator an animal that feeds on another animal.

Pupa the stage in an insect's life when it lives in a case as it changes from a caterpillar to an adult.

Rear to look after young until they are old enough to look after themselves.

Scale a small plate of tough material that protects the skin of fish and some reptiles.

Scrubland land with small bushes spaced out among herbaceous plants.

Seed ttiny capsule that contains a tiny plant and its food store.

Segment a part of a body. In earthworms the segments are all the same.

Shoot the part of a plant that grows above the soil. It includes the stem, leaves and flowers.

Spore a very tiny case that contains a part of a fungus, moss or fern, which can grow into a new fungus or plant.

Stalk a long thin support that holds up a flower or leaf.

Trade exchanging goods for other goods or for money.

ANSWERS TO THE ACTIVITIES AND QUESTIONS

Page 15 Habitats in summer

Activity: The picture could feature trees and flowers, with deer and their young under the trees. A close-up of a twig with a pupa on it and butterfly emerging could be in the foreground. Other butterflies could be above the flowers. Parent birds feeding their young could be featured on the ground in front of the flowers.

Page 17 Habitats in autumn

Activity: You should look for plants in flower and those that are producing fruit. Do not eat any of the fruits. You should also look for the shoots of herbaceous plants dying away and colour changes in the leaves of deciduous trees. Note when each tree begins to shed its leaves. Look for animals collecting or eating nuts and berries.

Page 19 Habitats in winter

Activity: The young birds learn to feed themselves. Birds may gather into flocks. Insects may hibernate as adults or stay in eggs and pupa through the winter. Mammals grow thicker coats of hair. Some animals eat a lot of food and become fatter before they hibernate and others make food stores to use later.

Page 25 Humans and habitats

Answer: People did not take too much food from any one place at the same time so the plants and animals were not destroyed. Today, habitats are being destroyed to make way for farms, towns, cities, roads, railways, airports, mines for coal and metal ores. Human actions have made Earth's atmosphere trap more heat, warming the planet and causing harm to habitats worldwide.

FURTHER INFORMATION

BOOKS TO READ

The Big Picture: Living Habitats by Jon Richards, Franklin Watts

Extreme Science: Magnificent Habitats by Rob Colson and Jon Richards, Wayland

Science Skills Sorted: Habitats by Anna Claybourne, Franklin Watts

World Feature Focus: Habitats by Rebecca Kahn, Franklin Watts

WEBSITES

Explore habitats and the natural world using the BBC's wildlife webpages.
www.bbc.co.uk/nature/habitats

Find out more about habitats and other facts about nature and conservation.
wildlife.durrell.org/kids/fun-factsheets/habitats-factsheet/

Learn more about food chains and habitats in savannah, tundra and woodland.
www.bbc.co.uk/bitesize/topics/zbnnb9q

Take a virtual tour of the 'Habitat' exhibition at the Smithsonian Gardens in Washington, DC.
gardens.si.edu/exhibitions/habitat

NOTE TO PARENTS AND TEACHERS:

Every effort has been made by the publisher to ensure that these websites contain no inappropriate or offensive material. However, because of the nature of the Internet, it is impossible to guarantee that the content of these sites will not be altered. We strongly advise that Internet access is supervised by a responsible adult.

INDEX

amphibians 11, 22

birds 5, 11, 13, 15, 17–23, 27
building (roads and buildings) 24–25

characteristics 11
climate change 25–26

earthworms 10

farming 24–25
fish 5, 11, 20–22
food chains 4–5, 22–23
fungi 17

habitats
    coral reef 5
    desert 11, 23
    forest 4, 22–23
    freshwater 4, 11, 20–21, 27
    grasslands 23
    mountain 7
    polar 22
    protecting habitats 26–27
    rainforest 23
    rocky 4, 6
    saltwater 11, 20
    scrubland 22
    soil 7, 10
    stone 4, 11
    tundra 22
    woodland 4, 7, 10–12, 17, 19, 23
hibernation 13, 17–19
humans 24–25

insects 10, 12–15, 18, 20–¬23, 27
invertebrates 10, 20 and see separate entries for insects, molluscs etc

keys, using 8–9

mammals 11, 13, 15–17, 19, 21–24
migration 18–19
mining 25–27
molluscs 10, 20–21

plankton 20–22
plants 4–12, 16–18, 20–23, 26–27
    conifers 6–7, 22
    deciduous plants 7, 14, 16–18
    evergreen plants 18
    ferns 6
    flowering plants 6–10, 12, 14
    fruits 12, 17, 23
    herbaceous plants 7, 12, 14, 16, 18
    mosses 4, 6
    seeds 7, 12, 17–19, 22
    spores 6, 17
    trees 7, 10–11, 13–19, 22–23, 26–27
    pollution 26

recycling 27
reptiles 11, 22

seasons 7, 12–19, 22–23

vertebrates 10–11

weather 5, 7, 12–19, 21–23, 25
worms 20